BARB FRYE

TRAINING METHODS THAT WORK

A Handbook For Trainers

Lois B. Hart, Ed.D.

CRISP PUBLICATIONS, INC.
Los Altos, California

TRAINING METHODS THAT WORK
A Handbook For Trainers

Lois B. Hart, Ed.D.

CREDITS
Editor: **Michael Crisp**
Layout and Composition: **Interface Studio**
Cover Design: **Carol Harris**
Artwork: **Ralph Mapson**

All rights reserved. No part of this book may be reproduced or transmitted in any form or by any means now known or to be invented, electronic or mechanical, including photocopying, recording, or by any information storage or retrieval system without written permission from the author or publisher, except for the brief inclusion of quotations in a review.

Copyright © 1991 by Crisp Publications, Inc.
Printed in the United States of America

English language Crisp books are distributed worldwide. Our major international distributors include:

CANADA: Reid Publishing, LTD., Box 7267, Oakville, Ontario Canada L6J 6L6. TEL: (416) 842-4428, FAX: (416) 842-9327

AUSTRALIA: Career Builders, P. O. Box 1051, Springwood, Brisbane, Queensland, Australia 4127. TEL: 841-1061, FAX: 841-1580

NEW ZEALAND: Career Builders, P. O. Box 571, Manurewa, Auckland, New Zealand. TEL: 266-5276, FAX: 266-4152

JAPAN: Phoenix Associates Co., Mizuho Bldg. 2-12-2, Kami Osaki, Shinagawa-Ku, Tokyo 141, Japan. TEL: 3-443-7231, FAX: 3-443-7640

Selected Crisp titles are also available in other languages. Contact International Rights Manager Tim Polk at (415) 949-4888 for more information.

Library of Congress Catalog Card Number 90-84925
Hart, Lois B.
Training Methods That Work
ISBN 1-56052-082-5

PREFACE

New trainers have so much to think about...their design, materials, and delivery...that often the training methods they use are inadequate or inappropriate. They rely on what they've previously experienced in training settings and perhaps on what they've read. Unfortunately, the result is that all too often trainers lecture too much, a common complaint of participants!

When a training program is successful and well received, participants' comments usually reveal that there was substantial interaction and variety. Clearly, learners respond better and learn more when a variety of training methods are used and enjoy the sessions more than just listening to a lecture.

Early in my career as a trainer, I did too much lecturing but soon realized that my training designs needed more variety. So over the years, I incorporated more methods into my programs...and the results and feedback from participants was dramatic.

Increasingly in the past few years, I've presented train-the-trainer workshops and developed resource books for trainers and group leaders.

The Rocky Mountain and Pikes Peak Chapters of the American Society of Training and Development recently asked me to conduct a workshop for those who wanted to know how to select, design, and deliver training methods. As I was designing this program, to my disappointment, I found that there was no single resource book available that covered training methods in the detail that these trainers wanted. That workshop led to this book.

Several people helped make this book more useful. Cheryl Wiles was there from the beginning suggesting the kinds of materials that less experienced trainers wanted in a resource book and critiquing the final product. My publisher, Michael Crisp and his editor, Kathleen Barcos, saw the need for this kind of book and helped me to make it come alive.

Lois B. Hart

i

CONTENTS

P A R T

I

Add Variety
To Your Training

VARIETY HELPS YOUR TRAINING

Training methods are the meat on the bones and the frosting on the cake of any training program design. Training methods give participants something to chew on. They also sweeten up any program.

This book provides you with a menu of seventeen tested training methods. These techniques help participants to learn about the concepts and skills you have outlined in your goals and objectives.

From the collection of methods found in this book, you can select those that introduce or reinforce a concept or skill. You can mix and match methods, combining them to ensure that more is learned. But most important, using these methods provides the variety necessary to make your training designs more interesting and more meaningful.

Another goal of this book is to increase your competence and confidence in selecting, designing, adapting, and implementing these training methods. As you review the material in this book, identify which methods you have the most confidence in and keep using them. Also identify which methods you are not familiar with. Study these, try them out, and evaluate their effectiveness. With practice, you will gain more confidence.

WHAT TRAINING METHODS SHOULD YOU USE?

The seventeen training methods described later in this book will provide the variety you need for your workshops. They were carefully selected from many sources. Authors of various methods often use different definitions and explanations that can add confusion. The purpose of this book is to provide a clear, yet comprehensive list of choices.

Dugan Laird in his book, *Approaches to Training and Development,** devoted one chapter to training methods. He introduced a duo-dimensional chart that compared each of his particular list of methods with the degree of learner participation and with the degree to which learners would determine the content.

Laird's system inspired the model for organizing the seventeen methods found in this book. The chart of the seventeen methods shown on page five compares each method to three criteria.

The first criteria is based on who determines the content: the trainer and/or the learners. The second criteria is based on the degree of participation—active or passive—taken by the learners. The third criteria for evaluating methods is based on which of three senses are utilized: sight, sound, or hands-on (psychomotor).

Familiarize yourself with this chart—it will help you to select just the right method for your training design. This chart will be referred to again in Part IV as each specific method is described in more detail.

SEVENTEEN METHODS

---

*Laird, Addison-Wesley 1978, p. 297

SEVENTEEN TRAINING METHODS

	Content Determined by		Learners' Role		Senses		
	Trainer	Learner	Passive	Active	Sight	Sound	Hands-on
STRUCTURED WARM-UP ACTIVITIES	✓			✓			✓
PRESENTATION	✓		✓		✓	✓	
READING	✓		✓		✓		
DEMONSTRATION	✓		✓	✓	✓	✓	✓
VIDEO/FILM	✓		✓		✓	✓	
NOTE-TAKING	BOTH		BOTH		✓		✓
DISCUSSION	BOTH		BOTH			✓	
QUESTIONNAIRES	✓		BOTH				✓
FISHBOWL	BOTH			✓		✓	
CASE STUDY	✓			✓		✓	✓
IN-BASKET/ CARD SORT	✓			✓			✓
ROLE PLAY	✓			✓			✓
ROLE PLAY A CASE STUDY	✓			✓			✓
GAMES	✓			✓	✓	✓	✓
CLINICS		✓		✓			✓
CRITICAL INCIDENTS		✓		✓			✓
STRUCTURED CLOSURE ACTIVITIES	✓			✓			✓

SELF ASSESSMENT

Now that you are familiar with these seventeen methods, check your expertise with each of them:

	I know very little about this one	I know this method but need to practice	I am proficient and able to teach it
STRUCTURED WARM-UP ACTIVITIES			
PRESENTATION			
READING			
DEMONSTRATION			
VIDEO/FILM			
NOTE-TAKING			
DISCUSSION			
QUESTIONNAIRES			
FISHBOWL			
CASE STUDY			
IN-BASKET/ CARD SORT			
ROLE PLAY			
ROLE PLAY A CASE STUDY			
GAMES			
CLINICS			
CRITICAL INCIDENTS			
STRUCTURED CLOSURE ACTIVITIES			

HOW TO USE THIS BOOK

Part II of this book provides you with a foundation of training principles and a learning model upon which you can select and use the seventeen training methods discussed. The Learning Cycle outlines the proper place for introducing activities and the role a trainer plays in conducting and processing them. Adult learning principles in training are reviewed.

Part III returns to the discussion of training methods starting with questions to use when selecting the appropriate method. There is a list of sources for exercises, however, most trainers wisely discover the need to adapt and/or write new ones, so those steps are outlined. Wise trainers always wonder about copyright issues so there is information on U.S. copyright law. The essential skills of introducing, conducting, and processing activities plus how to judge timing follows. Each method and new activity should be evaluated.

Part IV and the balance of the book cover seventeen specific training methods. They are presented in the same order as shown on the methods chart (page 5). They are sequenced from passive to more active in terms of learners' participation and from less learner involvement to more in determining content. Each method is then described in detail with steps outlined for preparing and utilizing the method.

THIS BOOK IS EASY TO USE!

PART

II

Using Training Methods:
A Foundation

THE FOUNDATION FOR USING TRAINING METHODS

Using training methods effectively requires a sound foundation of learning principles and a learning model.

Part I will first review the Learning Cycle by presenting a theoretical model that will help you understand the three stages learners go through and your role during each stage.

Next, adult learning principles will be presented. These form the basis for all training designs and methods. These principles also provide your frame of reference for working with adults in learning settings.

The final important perspective concerns the role of the facilitator in training. This facilitative role is a key to providing a quality program and optimizing learning.

THE LEARNING CYCLE

OVERVIEW

When you are selecting, adapting or writing training exercises, it is important to make your decision on which method to use based on a model of how people learn. This learning cycle includes three stages:

1. Presentation of the learning activity

2. The participants' response

3. Application to everyday life

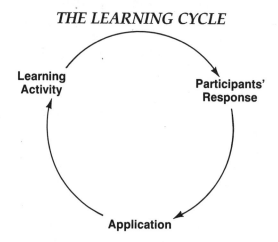

THE LEARNING CYCLE

Stage One: The Learning Activity

Initially, learners are involved in some activity that you have selected from the many learning methods and experiences available. This activity might be relatively passive like reading or observing a demonstration, or very active like solving a case study or participating in a role play.

The objectives may be very general like ''to explore...'' ''to examine...'' or ''to read...''; or very specific like ''to name the five causes of performance problems.''

The purpose of the learning activity is to encourage inductive learning through reading or deductive learning through experience. In either case, the learning activity provides the basis for understanding a concept or skill and a foundation for stage two of the learning cycle.

Stage Two: The Participants' Response

After the initial exposure to the learning activity, the participants are now ready to respond to what happened and perhaps to identify how they felt. This is a critical part of the learning cycle because it encourages learners to identify the impact of what they were exposed to in the first stage, to analyze both feelings and information, and to continue their focus on the experience or learning. This is all necessary to help the learner prepare for the application stage. Stage Two should not be rushed.

Various methods can be used to elicit participants' responses. A few successful ones include:

- Polling
- Rating
- Small group discussions
- Listing of responses on newsprint
- Interviewing partners
- Questioning
- Sentence completion

Stage Three: Application of Learning

Once the learners have thoroughly worked through Stage Two, they are now ready to move toward application of the learning to their own life and work. Out of the analysis, processing, and discussion done in Stage Two, participants can begin to make generalizations, draw conclusions, and transfer them to their everyday life. Learning now moves from the abstract to the concrete.

At this point, a review of the information, concepts, and theory is appropriate because it serves to augment what else has been learned in the other two stages.

Action plans and goal setting come in various forms, sometimes simply a verbal, short statement or at other times an elaborate and detailed plan. Some specific activities are presented later in this book.

Often, the learners' good intentions for applying learning are reinforced when they share their goals and plans with others, either those in this workshop group or with others back at work.

LEARNING CYCLE EXERCISE

Think back to a recent time when you were a participant in a training program so you can determine your part in the Learning Cycle:

Stage One: The Learning Activity

1. What were the stated objectives?
2. What activity was used to introduce the concept or skill?

Stage Two: The Participants' Responses

What did the trainer do to elicit responses from you and the other participants:

- Polling?
- Round robin?
- Small group discussions?
- Questioning?

Stage Three: Application of Learning

What was done that encouraged you to apply what you had learned?

- A review of the concepts or skill?
- Development of an action plan or goal setting?

ADULT LEARNING PRINCIPLES

OVERVIEW

Adult learning principles are important for you to learn and use as a trainer or training facilitator. If you use adult learning principles both to develop training designs and to facilitate your groups, you'll increase the likelihood that your adult group members will learn, be committed to the group's goals, and generate more solutions to problems.

DIFFERENCES BETWEEN CHILDREN AND ADULTS AS LEARNERS

CHILDREN	ADULTS
Rely on others to decide what is important to be learned	Decide for themselves what is important to be learned
Accept the information being presented at face value	Need to validate the information based on their beliefs and experiences
Expect that what they are learning will be useful in their long-term future	Expect that what they are learning is immediately useful
Have little or no experience upon which to draw—are relatively "clean slates"	Have much past experience upon which to draw—may have fixed viewpoints
Have little ability to serve as a knowledgeable resource to teacher or fellow classmates	Have significant ability to serve as a knowledgeable resource to the facilitator and group members
Are content centered	Are problem centered
Are less actively involved	Actively participate
Learn in an authority-oriented environment	Function best in a collaborative environment
Planning is teacher's responsibility	Share in planning

PRACTICE APPLYING ADULT LEARNING PRINCIPLES

Use the following checklist of the eight adult learning principles to evaluate if you are applying them to your workshop design:

DO I...

☐ Focus on "real world" problems?

☐ Emphasize how they can apply what happens in the group?

☐ Relate the group activities to their goals?

☐ Relate the materials to their past experiences?

☐ Allow debate and challenge of ideas?

☐ Listen to and respect the opinions of group members?

☐ Encourage members to share resources with you and each other?

☐ Treat everyone in adult-like manner?

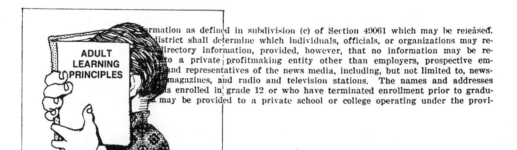

P A R T

III

Preparing and Using Training Methods

PREPARING AND USING TRAINING METHODS

With a sound foundation of training principles and the Learning Cycle in mind, you are now ready to select, adapt, write, conduct, and evaluate the training methods presented in Part IV.

This part of the book provides you with step-by-step guidelines for preparing and using the seventeen methods discussed.

When selecting from among the training methods, apply the nine key questions outlined on page 22 in order to select the most appropriate ones. When you are looking for exercises, case studies, role plays, and other structured activities, you can use the list of sources provided.

Since it is rare that you will find the perfect activity for your training, page 25 reviews the steps for adapting an exercise. Experienced trainers often write original exercises. A step-by-step guide on page 27 shows you how to do this.

Trainers are always concerned about how copyright law affects their use of other people's material. Trainers should also know how to protect their original work. Information on the U.S. copyright law is provided on page 29.

Once a method or exercise has been selected, adapted or written, trainers need to know how to facilitate the learning process. On page 31, facilitative techniques are covered in detail.

Judging the timing of methods and activities is always difficult so this special issue is covered on page 35.

Part III closes with a list of seven key questions to evaluate the effectiveness of a particular method.

SELECTING TRAINING METHODS

OVERVIEW

This book covers seventeen different training methods that can be incorporated into any training design. Of course the learning methods you select should fit the objectives of the training design. In addition, a variety of methods should be utilized to meet the variety of ways in which adults learn.

The chart on the facing page identifies how each training method meets each of three criteria:

1. Who determines the content? Is the content determined by the trainer or by the learners?

2. What role does the learner play? Is it passive or active?

3. Which of the three senses are utilized most? Sight? Sound? or Hands-on?

TRAINING METHODS

	Content Determined by		Learners' Role		Senses		
	Trainer	Learner	Passive	Active	Sight	Sound	Hands-on
STRUCTURED WARM-UP ACTIVITIES	✔			✔			✔
PRESENTATION	✔		✔		✔	✔	
READING	✔		✔		✔		
DEMONSTRATION	✔		✔		✔	✔	✔
VIDEO/FILM	✔		✔		✔	✔	
NOTE-TAKING	✔		✔		✔		✔
DISCUSSION	✔			✔		✔	
QUESTIONNAIRES	✔			✔			✔
FISHBOWL	✔			✔		✔	
CASE STUDY	✔			✔		✔	✔
IN-BASKET/ CARD SORT	✔			✔			✔
ROLE PLAY	✔			✔			✔
ROLE PLAY A CASE STUDY	✔			✔			✔
GAMES	✔			✔	✔	✔	✔
CLINICS	✔			✔			✔
CRITICAL INCIDENTS	✔			✔			✔
STRUCTURED CLOSURE ACTIVITIES							✔

SELECTING APPROPRIATE TRAINING METHODS

Choosing the most appropriate training methods depends first on utilizing the correct steps to develop a training design. A companion book to this one, *Developing Instructional Design*, by Geri McArtle, is available from your Crisp Publications distributor.

The steps to select the most appropriate training method include determining the needs of the learners, writing out objectives, identifying learning by knowledge, skills and attitudes, selecting specific methods and finally putting them into a sequence so a method can be established to evaluate the program.

NINE QUESTIONS

The following nine questions will help you clarify and select the most appropriate methods for your program:

1. On a scale of 1–10, how complex is the information or skill? The more complex the information or skill is, the more methods will be needed to ensure learning. For example, you might need to introduce reading material on the information, followed by a demonstration and discussion, then practice and more reading materials.

2. On a scale of 1–10, how resistant are the participants to what will be presented? Participants may be resistant to ''high touch'' activities or to certain subjects, such as technological ones.

3. How important is it that there is high participation? If your objective is to keep energy high or to have participants interact with one another, then you'll want methods that utilize high participation.

4. How much time is available? Since most activities tend to take longer than you think, be sure to select a method that will allow sufficient time for the activity, plus participants' response and application (as explained in the section on the Learning Cycle).

5. Does your overall selection of methods provide a variety of participation and senses? As mentioned earlier, people learn using different senses. Therefore using a variety of methods will ensure greater participation.

6. How confident are you in utilizing the particular method you are considering? Naturally you want to use the methods you feel most confident about. However, you might want to introduce one method in each of your designs that is relatively new to you so you can test its effectiveness and your ability to utilize it.

7. How much work is involved in preparing to use this method? For example, sometimes you won't have the time to write a case study so you might need to use a genetic version.

8. Could two or more methods be utilized together? For example, the questionnaire followed by a fishbowl works well. A guided discussion following a film is always essential.

9. Does the method require equipment or a room set-up that is readily available? Obviously it would be hard to use a video if you don't easily have access to the equipment (or know how to use it!).

SOURCES OF TRAINING EXERCISES

Fortunately, there are increasing numbers of sources from which to choose specific training exercises. The following lists some mail order sources:

American Society for Training &
    Development
1630 Duke St. Box
1443 Alexandria, VA 22313
703-683-8129

Crisp Publications, Inc.
95 First Street
Los Altos, CA 94022
415-949-4888

Human Resource Development Press
22 Amherst
Amherst, MA 01002
800-822-2801

Lakewood Publications Editors' Choice
50 South Ninth St.
Minneapolis, MN 55402
800-328-4329

Leadership Dynamics
875 Poplar Ave.
Boulder, CO 80304
303-440-0909

Organization Design and
    Development
HRD Quarterly
2002 Renaissance Blvd. Suite 100
King of Prussia, PA 19406
215-279-2002

The Training Store
Five South Miller Road
Harrisburg, PA 17109
800-222-9909

University Associates
8517 Production Avenue
San Diego, CA 92121
619-578-5900

SELECTING A TRAINING METHOD: EXERCISE

Think about one part of your workshop design (approximately one hour long) and select one or two methods. Then evaluate your selection by answering these questions:

1. How complex is the information or skill to be presented?

2. How resistant will the participants be to this method?

3. Is a high level of participation necessary?

4. If I use this method, will I have enough variety in the types of methods used throughout my design?

5. How confident am I in using this method?

6. How much work will it require to get ready to use this method?

7. Would this method work better if combined with another one?

8. How much time will be available and will it be enough time to use this method?

9. Does this method require any equipment or special room set-up?

ADAPTING AND WRITING EXERCISES

OVERVIEW

You will never find an exercise that fits your circumstances perfectly. It is very important to try to match the details in any exercise you use to the needs and objectives of your participants. Following are some guidelines on how to adapt an existing exercise and also on how to write an original one.

ADAPTING AN EXERCISE

1. Identify what you know about your participants including their roles in the organization, plus demographics on gender, race, ethnicity, and age.

   Also learn enough about the organization in which they work so you are familiar with its structure, unique culture, and "language".

2. Keeping your workshop objectives in mind, read over the closest existing exercise you can locate and note the details that participants may not identify with easily. Note which parts could be re-written so that participants could relate better to them.

3. Re-write those parts and details with your participants in mind.

4. Test it out whenever possible with people who are similar to your group of participants. Re-write as needed.

5. After using your exercise, evaluate its effectiveness and make notes.

PRACTICE: ADAPT AN EXERCISE

Select an exercise that needs adapting so that it will fit your participants' needs more appropriately.

Follow the guidelines on adapting an exercise found on page 25 and make changes in the exercise by completing the following:

ASSUMPTIONS I CAN MAKE ABOUT MY PARTICIPANTS:
(roles, demographics)

WHAT I KNOW ABOUT THE ORGANIZATION:
(structure, size, culture, vocabulary)

DETAILS AND PARTS TO BE CHANGED IN THE EXERCISE:

WRITING A NEW EXERCISE

1. Identify what you know about your participants including their roles in the organization and demographics on gender, race, ethnicity, and age.

   Also learn enough about the organization in which they work so you are familiar with its structure, unique culture, and "language."

2. Write your objective(s) based on the skills and/or principles you are covering.

3. Establish a situation or problem that illustrates the skill or principle.

4. Decide which training method or type of exercise you have most confidence in facilitating.

5. Write out the details of the chosen method or exercise. For example, with a role play you'll need to develop your characters with a name, role, and attitude. For a game or structured activity, you'll need rules.

6. Prepare an introduction to the exercise.

7. Outline each step.

8. Write out key questions for processing.

9. Prepare any handouts or other visuals.

10. Determine your room set-up, equipment, and supplies.

11. Determine about how many people you think this exercise will work with and how long you think it will take.

12. Test your exercise out whenever possible, with people who are similar to your participants, or minimally with a respected colleague. Refine details to reflect their feedback and response.

13. Evaluate how effective it was. Make notes.

WRITING YOUR EXERCISE*

Title _____

Participants _____ **Group Size** _____

Objectives _____

_____

_____

Type of Training Method _____

Time Needed _____ **Room Set Up** _____

Supplies/Equipment

_____   _____

_____   _____

Materials/Handouts

_____   _____

_____   _____

Steps for Introducing, Conducting & Processing

_____

_____

_____

_____

_____

_____

Variations

_____

_____

Resources

_____

Notes

_____

_____

_____

*Note: This page may be reproduced without further permission.

COPYRIGHT LAW

Throughout your career as a trainer or as a manager who is involved in training, you probably will create many workshop designs, exercises, handouts, articles and reports. Thanks to the U.S. Copyright Law of 1978, as an author you possess certain rights automatically upon creation of your materials.

At other times, you have probably drawn upon others' work to enhance your own ideas. Because borrowing ''facts'' from other published works is a common practice in the training industry you should be aware of the law that protects both your work and that of others.

COPYRIGHT PROTECTION FOR AUTHORS

Your training materials are automatically protected upon creation. With this new copyright law, no registration with the Copyright Office is necessary to secure copyright privileges although it is recommended. You should always show a credit line that the material is original and protect it by displaying a © symbol, with your name and the year the work was completed.

This protection covers both published and unpublished works and exists to protect ''original works of authorship'' when they become fixed in a tangible form of expression. The law gives the copyright owner (or others authorized by him/her) the right to do the following:

1. Reproduce the work in copies

2. Distribute copies to the public for sale

3. Produce derivative works (a translation, adaptation or dramatization) based upon some previously copyrighted work

FAIR USE OF COPYRIGHTED MATERIALS

In the interest of knowledge, Congress and the courts decided it would be best if current authors could have free access to the facts, ideas, and even words found in earlier authors' works.

The principle of ''Fair Use'' allows you to take *facts* freely, however, the *expression* belongs to the author. By judicious paraphrasing, authors are using the facts without using the author's expression. There are no concrete rules on fair use of paraphrasing partly because of conflicting court rulings.

COPYRIGHT LAW (Continued)

Copyright law does not define the exact limits of fair use but there are a few guidelines you should use before publishing copyrighted material:

1. Is it going to be used for profit?

2. What is the nature of the work from which quotes are taken?

3. Could it cause economic damage?

4. Relative to the total material, what percentage would be used?

There is no exact number of words you can use without asking permission; however, a good rule of thumb is 300 words if it is from a book-length work, two lines from poetry, or 10% from a letter.

Keep these factors in mind and use your own good judgment. If you have a question, ask! Otherwise you could risk serious charges of copyright infringement.

Both as an author and as a user of copyrighted materials, it is your responsibility to learn copyright law as it applies to you. Remember, copyright law is a two-way protection—it protects your work as well as others.

For additional copyright information call the Copyright Office Hotline at (202) 287-9100 or write the Copyright Office LM455, Library of Congress, Washington, D.C. 20559 and ask for Circular 2, ''Publications on Copyright''.

EXERCISE: How Well Do You Know the Copyright Law?

T or F 1) It is all right to borrow ''facts'' from another published work.

T or F 2) My training materials are automatically protected upon creation.

T or F 3) As a copyright owner, I can reproduce and sell my work.

T or F 4) The principle of *Fair Use* does not allow me to paraphrase another author's work.

T or F 5) There is an exact number of words you can use without asking permission.

---

1) False. There are restrictions on ''borrowing'' from copyrighten works.

2) True. However, it helps to also register your creation with the Copyright Office in Washington.

3) True. You can reproduce, sell and produce derivations of your own copyrighted works.

4) False. You can paraphrase facts but the original expression belongs to the the author.

5) False. There is no set number of words, however, a good rule of thumb is 300 words if it is from a book-length work.

INTRODUCE, CONDUCT, AND PROCESS TRAINING METHODS AND ACTIVITIES

OVERVIEW

A properly selected, adapted or written, training method or activity is only as good as how it is introduced, conducted, and processed. These three skills are critical to ensure optimal learning.

The skill of processing is especially critical with experiential activities such as simulations (case studies, role plays, and clinics).

INTRODUCING AN ACTIVITY

1. Give a purpose and objective for the upcoming activity.

2. Re-arrange furniture and re-group participants as needed but as smoothly as possible. Wait until everyone is settle before proceeding.

3. Elicit information from participants as to what experience or knowledge they already have on the topic.

4. Provide definitions of all terms to be used.

5. Give directions that not only explain the activity but tell what will happen afterwards. For example, will the data on the questionnaire be shared and if so, how? Will everyone be paired up to replicate the demonstration that they are about to see?

6. Distribute any printed instructions and read them together before starting the activity. If you will be giving only oral directions, be sure to have everyone's attention before starting.

7. Answer questions before continuing.

8. Demonstrate rules or procedures.

9. If you are using an activity that requires them to participate, always be the first to share or try it out.

10. Roam around the room to determine if everyone knows what to do.

CONDUCTING THE ACTIVITY

1. Expect some confusion and/or frustration. Some of this helps to encourage problem solving and learning.

2. Be available to re-explain the directions.

3. Stick to your role as the facilitator. Don't try to play a game and also guide it at the same time.

4. Be observant at all times as to how individuals and groups are working on the problems, how well they work together and when they need prodding or help from you. As they are working, take clues from them if and how you should intervene.

5. Remind them of the passing of time especially if there's a deadline to complete an activity.

6. Judge when to stop an activity and move on to the processing stage.

PROCESSING THE ACTIVITY

1. Plan on using about as much time to process an experiential activity as it took to conduct it.

2. If you used only some participants to do a demonstration or role play, get feedback from them first before eliciting feedback from observers.

3. Prepare and ask questions that:

   • review or summarize what happened in the activity or what they learned

   • identify feelings that occurred at different points in their learning experience

   • identify choices they considered and how they made a particular decision

   • point out different roles people played during the experience

   • identify any patterns in the information, behaviors or attitudes

   • reveal conflicts and other unfinished business

   • highlight the possibility of trying out alternative behaviors

4. Record participants' feedback and ideas on the flipchart. Use a participant as recorder to keep you free to lead the discussion.

5. Expect differences of opinion and perceptions. Enforce your guidelines on giving each other feedback so all ideas are accepted and personal attacks do not occur.

6. Be sure to complete the learning cycle and help participants relate the learning experience back to the lesson's objectives and to their own real situations.

7. Ask for feedback on your learning activity so you can evaluate its effectiveness.

PRACTICE: PREPARE TO INTRODUCE AND PROCESS AN ACTIVITY

Select an activity you want to use in your training design and complete the following.

Name of activity: _____

1. Write out the purpose for using this activity.

2. Write out your definitions of all terms you will be using.

3. Write out the directions for this activity.

4. Write questions you will ask after they have experienced the activity.

TACKLING YOUR TIMING

Inexperienced trainers often ask ''How much time should I allow for doing an exercise or activity?'' or ''When do I know if the group has taken enough time to discuss a topic fully?''

Judging your timing is very intuitive. It requires patience so decide to be patient with the group and its process. You may know where you want them to go and how they might get there, but you need to patiently guide them in that direction. If you rush them, they may not fully explore an issue or learn how to resolve their problems.

Trust your instinct. Usually your first impression or reaction is right, so if you feel it's time to stop—listen and act.

HOW TO JUDGE TIMING WHEN USING METHODS AND ACTIVITIES

If you're using an exercise found in a training resource book, suggested timelines are usually given. If you've selected an activity that doesn't have a timeline, calculate how much time you think each part might take, then add about 25% more. If you are still unsure, ask another facilitator if they think you've calculated accurately.

Do a dress rehearsal of the activity to help you test the amount of time it might take participants to read directions and do what is asked of them.

If you are doing an important activity with the group and they are working well on it, don't rush them. Instead, be flexible about the remainder of your plans with them. Be ready to trim or drop certain components of your design. It is better to trim your plans than to rush them too much.

Be sure to leave about equal time for participants to do an activity and for you to process the experience with them.

Ask the group how the timing is for them. They'll let you know if it is too fast or too slow or just right.

When the timing feels right, grab the opportunity. Sometimes, ideas that were ruled out earlier may now be accepted.

When desperation and frustration peak, it is often the best time for you to suggest a solution that incorporates the best of all of the ideas offered. The members probably realize they are stuck and may welcome your consensus-testing.

If the group cannot finish within the amount of time available in that particular session, review what they have accomplished and identify any work they can do between sessions. At the beginning of the next session, review what they have done, and suggest any changes in methods or activities.

After using one of these methods or activities, make notes on how much time it took so you'll be ready to use it the next time.

EVALUATING METHODS AND EXERCISES

Just as it is important to evaluate your whole workshop, you also need to continually evaluate particular methods and exercises you've used. This is especially true when you're trying out something new and would like feedback on its effectiveness.

You could do a self-evaluation or ask some of these questions of the participants:

1. Did the method or activity achieve the objective(s)?

_____

_____

2. Were the directions clear and concise?

_____

_____

3. Were the process questions sufficient in number and clearly understood?

_____

_____

4. Was enough time alloted for this activity?

_____

_____

5. Was this activity in the most appropriate place in the training design?

_____

_____

6. How receptive were participants to this activity?

_____

_____

7. How could this method or activity be adapted for future use?

_____

_____

P A R T

IV

Seventeen Training Methods That Work

SEVENTEEN TRAINING METHODS THAT WORK

The remainder of this book outlines in detail how to use each of seventeen training methods. As recommended earlier in Part I, use a variety of methods in each of your training designs. This will help you to successfully achieve your learning objectives.

As you again review the chart of the seventeen methods that are covered, assess your experience with each. Perhaps star those in which you have the most confidence and check those that you need to utilize more often.

For each method described there is an overview, a definition, and a detailed guideline plus a list of variations and resources.

METHOD	PAGE
1. STRUCTURED WARM-UP ACTIVITIES	42
2. THE PRESENTATION	43
3. READING MATERIALS	49
4. DEMONSTRATIONS	51
5. VIDEO AND FILMS	53
6. NOTE-TAKING	55
7. DISCUSSIONS	57
8. QUESTIONNAIRES	63
9. THE FISHBOWL	65
10. CASE STUDIES	67
11. IN-BASKET AND CARD SORTS	70
12. ROLE PLAYS	72
13. ROLE PLAYING A CASE STUDY	77
14. GAMES AND OTHER STRUCTURED ACTIVITIES	78
15. CLINICS	80
16. THE CRITICAL INCIDENTS	81
17. STRUCTURED CLOSURE ACTIVITIES	82

METHOD 1: STRUCTURED WARM-UP ACTIVITIES

OVERVIEW

Getting your workshop off on the right foot is essential. Using structured activities at the beginning of the training design ensures that the participants get involved right away, increases their energy and interest, and perhaps gives an early introduction to a key idea or skill that will be developed later. This method actively involves participants—they enjoy these hands on experiences.

GUIDELINES

1. Review your sources for an appropriate structured activity that fits your workshop objectives. As needed, adapt the details or write one that fits your participants' background.

2. Prepare the room and divide the participants into groups as directed.

3. Explain the purpose of the activity and review the directions.

4. Participants complete the activity.

5. Tie the purpose of the activity into the workshop objectives and design.

SOURCES

- Write your own activity following the guidelines provided in this book.

- Other reference books are exclusively devoted to warm-up activities:

  Saying Hello: Getting Your Group Started, by Lois Hart, Leadership Dynamics.

  Encyclopedia of Icebreakers, University Associates.

- Some training reference books will have sections devoted to warm-up activities.

METHOD 2: THE PRESENTATION

You will need to make a presentation so participants will have essential background information. Whether or not your presentation is five or fifty minutes long, you need to prepare and present it properly.

The content for the presentation is determined by you, based on your analysis of the participants' knowledge of the topic. Participants play a passive role generally absorbing the information.

DIFFERENCES BETWEEN FACILITATION AND GIVING A PRESENTATION	
FACILITATION	**PRESENTATIONS**
Purpose: To lead a group in its discussion To accomplish a task or solve a problem	To inform, report, instruct, motivate, persuade or entertain
Relationship to Group Members: The facilitator encourages members to participate fully and interface with one another continually	Usually the presentation is completed and then questions are asked
Size of Group Ideally 6–15	Any size

SIMILARITIES BETWEEN FACILITATION AND GIVING A PRESENTATION

The facilitator and presenter must be well prepared and thoroughly versed in the topics covered.

Knowledge of the group members is needed; this is obtained with an audience analysis.

A presenter needs to know how to handle questions as much as a facilitator would, however, the facilitator would ask questions of the group members as well as answer their questions.

PRACTICE: ADAPTING A WARM-UP ACTIVITY

1. Identify what you know about your participants and their organization (its structure, unique culture, and ''language'').

2. Compare what you've diagnosed in step one with an activity you are considering using for a warm-up. What doesn't quite fit your diagnosis and objectives? Note the part(s) that participants may not identify with easily. Note which parts could be re-written so that participants could relate better to them.

3. Re-write those parts and details. Either expand or reduce parts to fit the time you have alloted for this activity.

4. Try it out, evaluate its effectivenss and re-write as needed.

SIX STEPS TO PREPARE FOR A PRESENTATION

There are six steps to prepare for a presentation:

1. Determine your objectives for the presentation.

2. Analyze your audience.

3. Prepare a preliminary outline or plan.

4. Select and/or prepare visual aids.

5. Finalize the presentation outline and details.

6. Practice!

STEP 1: Determine your objectives for the presentation

In order to determine your objectives for giving this presentation, answer the following questions:

- Who suggested that the presentation should be done? (you? your boss?)

- When and where will it happen?

- Is your presentation a part of a longer design? If yes, what precedes or follows yours?

- How much do you know about the topic?

- Should the presentation be technical, theoretical, or practical?

- Why are you giving this presentation?

Write out a short goal statement that outlines the purpose of the presentation:

SIX STEPS TO PREPARE FOR A PRESENTATION (Continued)

STEP 2: Analyze your audience

The second step requires you to analyze your audience so the presentation can be geared to them. In order to do this, answer these questions:

- How much do they already know about your topic?

- What is their attitude toward the topic? (hostile? approving?)

- Why are they attending this presentation? (volunteer? mandatory?)

- What is their level of vocabulary relative to what you will present?

- How open-minded are they (eager? neutral? resistant?)

- What are some presentation techniques that might gain their attention?

- What are some presentation techniques that might get negative reactions from them?

STEP 3: Prepare a preliminary outline or plan

You are now ready to prepare a preliminary outline or plan basing it on everything you know so far about the participants.

Outline the main ideas you want to convey first. Consider putting each main idea on a separate self-adhesive note and then arrange them in approximate order for presentation. At this point, you could type your preliminary plan onto a word processor.

Make additional notes on ideas or examples that would support each main idea.

STEP 4: Select and/or prepare visual aids

For each main idea, think about using visual aids that could present the information more clearly or that would support what you will be presenting.

Which form of visual aid would be best to use or can you develop?

Video   Film   Flip Charts   Transparencies   Handouts

STEP 5: Finalize the presentation outline with details

Now you are ready to finalize your outline. First make sure that your points are in a logical order. Indicate in your notes where you will use your visual aids. Also indicate in the outline when you are willing to pause and answer questions.

Next determine how you will introduce your presentation. Some choices include:

- Direct statement of what will be presented and why it is important to your audience.

- Indirect opening using something that is of vital interest to your audience and would lead into your topic.

- Vivid example or comparison that leads into your topic.

- A strong quotation that relates to your topic.

- Important statistics.

- A story that illustrates what you are about to say.

Last, plan how you will summarize and close your presentation. It is important to restate your main ideas. End with a positive, direct appeal for action or vividly review the purpose of your presentation. Sometimes a final example, quotation or story works well.

STEP 6: Practice! Practice! Practice!

Do a practice session based on the length of your presentation, how familiar you are with the material, and your level of confidence.

Stand before a mirror and tape record your presentation or find a colleague who will sit through your practice session and give you feedback.

PREPARING FOR YOUR NEXT PRESENTATION

☑ **STEP 1**—Write a goal for your presentation:

☑ **STEP 2**—Analyse your audience:

Who are they?

What do they know and need to know?

☑ **STEP 3**—Prepare a preliminary outline that covers the important points you want to cover:

☑ **STEP 4**—Make a list of any visual aids you'll need:

☑ **STEP 5**—Add details to your outline:

Write out an introduction:

Write out your closing statement:

METHOD 3: READING MATERIALS

OVERVIEW

Reading materials can enhance learning as long as they are relevant and their purpose is clearly understood. The learners' roles are certainly more passive and rely only on sight. The positive impact of reading is increased when the reading material is relevant to participants' own situations, at their reading level, and done in conjunction with other learning methods.

GUIDELINES

1. Select the reading materials.

Too often, participants' notebooks are packed with copies of articles that are hard to read, too long, and often not totally relevant. This is the lazy, and often illegal, way to provide readings. It would be better to either select one or two absolutely relevant and clearly written articles than to overload participants with excessive materials. Your other choice is to re-write the materials to fit your program's content and write it in a style that can be more easily utilized.

2. When should the reading be introduced?

Beforehand: Sometimes you'll want participants to do some reading before coming to your program, especially if this background information is essential to their understanding of the content you plan to cover. Many people will not do the assigned reading; however, this can be mitigated if your selections are both short and readable. Explain that they must read these materials before the program starts.

During: Reading can provide a break from the group's dynamics as well as an opportunity for participants to get an overview preceding more group involvement. Be prepared for the variation in reading speeds of participants. Request that those who finish first remain quiet or slip out of the room for a break.

After: Suggested reading after your program often has little usefulness unless it is somehow tied into other follow-up activities. Most people will not do this follow-up reading unless they are truly excited about the materials.

READING MATERIALS: GUIDELINES
(Continued)

3. Introduce the purpose and process.

Explain why you think that reading this particular material will help them. Also tell them how you plan to have them use what they've learned in the follow-up activities you have planned. For example, the group will be discussing the major points, doing a case study, re-grouping to brainstorm solutions or perhaps taking a test.

4. Guided reading

You can help them to focus on what they read by providing a few key questions they will be asked to answer after finishing their reading. You could give them a handout with these questions.

5. Follow-up

Reading should not be done in isolation of other training methods because its purpose is diminished. Tie the reading into other learning activities and on-the-job application.

EXERCISE

Match these objectives with when materials should be read:

	Materials should be read		
	Before	During	Afterwards
To provide background	____	____	____
To reinforce learning	____	____	____
To supplement activities and presentations	____	____	____
To save time	____	____	____
To fill in time	____	____	____
To tie into other learning experiences	____	____	____

METHOD 4: DEMONSTRATIONS

OVERVIEW

Demonstrations are a powerful training method because participants utilize all their senses.

Demonstrations bring alive whatever points you are trying to make. Participants can experience an idea or technique. Demonstrations are essential when you are trying to teach a psychomotor procedure or operation. They work well also when you want to communicate better, discipline someone, or work with customers.

GUIDELINES

1. Prepare carefully!

Think through every step of the demonstration. Gather all of the materials you'll need to use and check any equipment out before hand. Set up the stage for the demonstration so that everyone will be able to see.

2. Explain the purpose

Clearly explain the purpose of the demonstration and direct participants' attention to follow certain steps. Let them know in advance if they will be expected to try out what is demonstrated.

3. Step-by-Step

Present each part of your demonstration step-by-step in small sequential steps.

4. Practice

Provide an opportunity for participants to practice, ideally at the end of each step of the demonstration. Reinforce their success and give helpful feedback when they don't perform exactly as they were shown in the demonstration.

DEMONSTRATION EXERCISE:

Prepare a demonstration by imagining that you need to teach someone how to handle a customer who phones in a complaint.

1. What would be the purpose of this demonstration?

2. What equipment would be needed?

3. Write out a common complaint a customer might have.

4. Write out the steps for demonstrating how to handle a customer complaint.

METHOD 5: VIDEO AND FILMS

OVERVIEW

Videotapes and films have particular advantages in learning experiences. These two visual aids help to stimulate interest and motivate participants to try new behaviors. The content can provide illustrations and models for the ideas and skills you are presenting in your workshop.

Although participants are passive as they view a video or film, this method is combined with a discussion so they become active.

STEPS FOR USING VIDEO/FILM IN TRAINING

STEP	DESCRIPTION
1. **Prepare for showing**	• Check that the videotape or film is the correct size for the available equipment. • Preview and identify the important points you want group members to get from viewing the video or film. • Try out the equipment and check lighting levels. If you will be asking the group members to take notes, adjust lighting plans accordingly.
2. **Provide instructions**	• Tell participants what they will see and why. • Instruct the group what to do during the film (take notes, watch for certain examples). • Tell them what they will do after the film (discuss what they saw, complete an exercise).
3. **Play the video/film**	• Adjust lighting. • Start video/film and adjust picture and volume. • Monitor their reactions to the video/film.
4. **Present/summarize major points**	• At the end of the videotape/film, have them discuss their reactions. • Summarize the key points you want group members to retain from the video/film.

VIDEO/FILM EXERCISE:

Select a video or film that you might use in your workshop. Preview it and answer these questions:

1. How could I introduce this video or film?

2. List some questions you might ask that would follow-up the viewing of the video or film:

METHOD 6: NOTE-TAKING

OVERVIEW

Whether or not you provide directions or handouts to participants for taking notes, many will do so automatically. These people may be the kind of learners who need to first hear the information, see it in any visual aids you provide and then see it again in the form of their notes. Other participants find note-taking a nuisance or unnecessary and seem to be able to listen and learn.

There are occasions when note-taking can be very helpful, for instance, when you are explaining a complicated procedure or you cover several critical steps or guidelines that they will need to remember.

TYPES

Free form: Most people remember taking notes of this type when they were in high school and college. The learner merely takes notes according to what they think they are hearing. This type depends heavily on the ability of the speaker or trainer to present information in an organized fashion so people can write notes that are useful.

Topical Outline: A more commonly used form of note-taking in training is to provide an outline of key words or topics on a handout and participants fill in the blank spaces with details.

Matrix: This is a variation of the topical outline when you provide a matrix with the two dimensions labeled and participants fill in the blanks. The matrix works well with material that compares and contrasts information.

GUIDELINES

1. Prepare a handout

As you prepare your design and activities, decide if a handout would enhance learning and encourage note-taking. Select the type that fits your objectives.
- Title the handout (perhaps with the date).
- Use bold type headings and leave plenty of space for notes to be taken.
- Add any pertinent footnotes or references.

2. Using the handouts

Let participants know if you are providing a handout on which they can take notes...before they start taking notes.

Explain the purpose for taking notes.

NOTE-TAKING REVIEW:

Name the three types of note-taking:

1. _____

2. _____

3. _____

Prepare a handout that only outlines the main points you will make during a mini-presentation in your workshop. Give it a title. Leave plenty of space for participants to take notes while you do the presentation.

MAPSON

METHOD 7: DISCUSSIONS

OVERVIEW

Discussion is probably used most frequently by trainers, however, it isn't learned quickly. The art of questioning takes lots of preparation and practice.

Discussions between the facilitator and participants and those among participants are a useful experience because the learners can take a more active role, help to determine more of the content to be discussed, and utilize more of their senses.

TYPES

Structured: The facilitator prepares a list of questions to be discussed based on defined objectives for holding this discussion. The content is more carefully controlled by the nature of the questions asked.

Free Form: This type is used when participants need to air their feelings and opinions. The facilitator needs to announce the purpose of this kind of discussion, explain ground-rules and carefully monitor the process. Here the participants take more control of the content of the discussion.

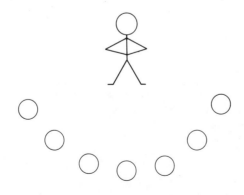

METHOD 7: DISCUSSIONS (Continued)

QUESTIONING SKILLS

Questions play a major role in facilitating discussions. Questions are used to:

• help you determine what participants already know about a topic so you can focus on what they need to learn.

• invite participation and involvement in the group process.

• provide you with feedback about how the experience is being received.

There are three skills associated with the questioning process. They are:

> **1.** Asking questions of the participants.
>
> **2.** Handling their answers to your questions.
>
> **3.** Responding to their questions.

ASKING QUESTIONS

Asking questions effectively is one of the most important skills you can develop. It means selecting the right type of question, phrasing it so it elicits the response you are after and then directing the question appropriately.

TYPES OF QUESTIONS

There are two basic types of questions from which to choose—open questions and closed questions.

TYPE OF QUESTION	DESCRIPTION	EXAMPLE
Closed	• Requires a one-word answer • Closes off discussion • Usually begins with ''is,'' ''can,'' ''how many,'' ''does'' • Use to guide or control	"Does everyone understand the changes we've discussed?"
Open	• Requires more than a ''yes'' or ''no'' answer • Stimulates thinking • Creates involvement • Elicits discussion • Usually begins with ''what,'' ''how,'' ''when,'' or ''why''	"What ideas do you have for explaining the changes to our customers?"

PHRASING QUESTIONS

Once you have decided on the type of question you will use, you need to determine how you will phrase it. There are important considerations in phrasing questions so that the participant focuses on the precise information you are trying to obtain.

GUIDELINES FOR PHRASING QUESTIONS

DO	DON'T
• Ask clear, concise questions covering a single issue.	• Ask rambling, ambiguous questions covering multiple issues.
• Ask reasonable questions based on what they can be expected to know at this point.	• Ask questions that are too difficult for the majority of them to answer.
• Ask challenging questions that provoke thought.	• Ask questions that are too easy and provide no opportunity for thinking.
• Ask honest, relevant questions—that direct them to logical answers.	• Ask ''trick'' questions designed to fool them.

DIRECTING QUESTIONS

The final consideration in asking effective questions is how to direct your question. There are two ways to direct questions:

1. To the group, or

2. To a specific individual

CHOOSING HOW TO DIRECT QUESTIONS

IF YOU WANT TO...	THEN...
Stimulate thinking—	direct the question to the group.
Allow them to respond voluntarily or avoid putting an individual on the spot—	ask a question like: "What experiences have you had on this issue?"
Stimulate one person to think and respond—	direct the question to that individual.
Tap the known resources of an "expert" in the group—	direct the question to her: "Mary, you have had a lot of experience in applying these regulations with customers. What would you do in this case?"

REVIEW: YOUR QUESTIONING SKILLS:

1. What is the value of asking "Open" questions vs. "Closed" ones?

2. Why shouldn't you ask "trick" questions?

3. Directing a question to the whole group will...

4. How can you respond to a partially correct question?

5. How can you reinforce a correct answer?

6. When should you defer a question addressed to you?

METHOD 7: DISCUSSIONS (Continued)

HANDLING ANSWERS TO QUESTIONS

The second skill associated with the questioning process involves the way in which you handle the answers to your questions. To ensure maximum learning in your group, you need maximum participation by all. Your answer has an impact not only on the individual but also on the amount of future participation you will receive from everyone.

Some ways to handle answers that will maintain a high level of participation are:

- Use positive reinforcement for correct answers.

- Acknowledge the effort of the respondent, regardless of whether the answer was right or wrong.

- Minimize potential embarrassment for wrong or incomplete answers.

TIPS FOR HANDLING ANSWERS		
IF THE ANSWER IS:		
Correct	**Incorrect**	**Partly Correct**
Use positive reinforcement	• Acknowledge the effort.	• Reinforce the correct portion.
Examples: "Yes." "Good point." "That's right."	**Then** • Redirect the question to others or answer it yourself.	**Then** • Redirect the question to the same person, to another, or answer it yourself.
	Examples: • "I can see how you might come up with that. Who else has an idea?"	**Examples:** • "You're on the right track. What other ideas do you have?"
	• "That's not exactly what I was looking for. What I was looking for was _____."	• "That's one good point, Joe. Who else has some ideas?"

RESPONDING TO QUESTIONS

The third skill associated with the questioning process involves responding to questions from the group. Questions provide an opportunity to enhance the learning for the group as well as for the individual asking the question. Your response to questions also affects whether they feel free to ask future questions during the group.

There are three acceptable ways to respond to questions. They are:

1. Provide the answer yourself.

2. Redirect the question back to the person.

3. Defer the question.

RESPONDING TO QUESTIONS

DO THE FOLLOWING	WHEN:
Provide the answer yourself.	• You are the only person who can provide the answer.
Redirect the question back to the same person or to another one.	• There is a high probability that the person will be able to come up with the correct answer.
Defer the question.	• The question is beyond the scope of the group.
	• The question cannot be handled in the allotted time frame.
	• The answer will be provided by material covered later on.
	• You need time to get the correct answer and get back to them.

METHOD 8: QUESTIONNAIRES

OVERVIEW

Questionnaires are prepared by the trainer to gather information on a particular subject. A set of questions are developed that measure a person's level of knowledge, attitudes or performance or analyzes an organization's conditions or productivity. The questionnaires can also be used for self-assessment by the individual who filled it out.

The participants' role is passive but can become more active if combined with another method like the fishbowl or discussion.

DEFINITIONS

The following terms are often used in training, perhaps interchangeably, which can cause confusion. These definitions are from Webster's *1989 New World Dictionary:*

Instrument: measures conditions, performance, position

Survey: a detailed study or inspection using a questionnaire, observation or analyzing data

Test: a set of questions to determine a person's knowledge, abilities or aptitudes

Questionnaire: gathers information on a subject using a set of questions; often asked of several people

For training purposes, the word *questionnaire* has been chosen because it encompasses the purpose and procedures of the other terms.

QUESTIONNAIRES (Continued)

GUIDELINES

1. Determining Your Purpose

Determine your purpose in either developing or selecting a particular questionnaire by answering these questions:

Will it be used as a stand-alone training activity?

Will it be used to test participants' knowledge?

Will it be used to help them get interested in the workshop topic?

2. Utilizing a Questionnaire

Clearly explain to participants the purpose of the questionnaire. Let them know in advance if they will be expected to share the information with others and in what form (in small groups or large group discussion).

Read the directions and answer any questions. Remind them that usually a first response to a question is the most accurate so suggest that they don't ponder too much.

Insist on quiet until everyone has finished. At one point you might ask how many people need more time to complete the questionnaire.

3. Follow-up

Proceed to the activity you planned as follow-up. This could include:

• forming small groups where people talk about their responses

• a large group discussion

• polling of responses and recording them on the flipchart

• holding a fishbowl discussion

METHOD 9: THE FISHBOWL

OVERVIEW

The fishbowl is just another form of discussion, but in this instance some of the participants form an inner circle where they discuss a topic while the remaining participants listen and observe. This method actively involves the participants because the content is partially determined by them.

GUIDELINES

1. Choose a topic that will be of interest to everyone. It might be the questionnaire's topic or a problem participants mentioned earlier. Prepare some questions that can be used for a discussion.

2. Determine how your group will be divided. For instance, divide by roles: men vs. women or managers vs. sales people or divide by experience or a division based on polarized attitudes.

3. Explain the purpose of a fishbowl and how it will be conducted.

4. Arrange a circle of chairs for those who are in the "fishbowl," with a ring of chairs for observers around the outside.

5. Ask the selected people to join you in the inner circle. Give instructions to the outer circle that they should be making notes on the points that are being discussed. They must remain absolutely quiet even though they will be tempted to talk among themselves!

6. Conduct the discussion for the designated period of time. Encourage participation by everyone in the inner circle.

7. When the time is up, switch groups so that those who had been listening are now in the "fishbowl."

8. When the second round's time is up, provide an opportunity for de-briefing. You could do this by forming one large group and sharing observations and areas of agreement/disagreement. Or you could form small groups of four made up of two people from each of the original sets of groups.

THE FISHBOWL (Continued)

VARIATIONS

1. The fishbowl method can also be used to observe group process and roles. In this case, the topic is less important although it should be one that those in the discussion can relate to and discuss. The outer circle is asked to observe:

    Who speaks and who remains quiet?

    What other roles do individuals play?

    How often does the discussion drift?

    What non-verbal signals did you see?

    How were conflicts handled?

2. The fishbowl also works well when your group is large and you want to hold a discussion with representatives from smaller groups. In this instance, form small groups where they discuss the topic, listing their concerns and clarifying the issues. They select a representative who goes into the fishbowl to represent their group's position. After a short period of time, the representatives return to their group, get feedback and discuss any change in their position. This process can be repeated several times until a resolution is found. The representatives can be rotated among the members of each small group.

METHOD 10: CASE STUDIES

OVERVIEW

The case study is a printed description of a problem situation with sufficient detail for participants to determine appropriate action they might take. The case study simulates reality, draws upon participants' experiences and knowledge, and involves them more actively in the learning process and forces them to apply theory to practice.

Usually, you will prepare the case study; however, you can involve participants in determining the content.

GUIDELINES

1. Review your sources for an appropriate case study that fits your objectives. As needed, adapt the details of the case study or write a case that fits your participants' problems or those of the organization.

2. Divide the participants into groups of four to six.

3. Explain the purpose of using a case study and read the directions.

4. Individuals follow the directions, read each case and rank the alternative responses.

5. In small groups, participants hold a discussion of their rankings. You may want them to reach consensus on a group ranking or merely hold a discussion on their rationale for their rankings.

6. Conduct a discussion with the total group, polling information from each group, perhaps tallying group rankings on the flipchart. Tie the questions you ask to the objectives of your lesson. Follow the guidelines on how to process an exercise.

CASE STUDIES (Continued)

VARIATIONS

1. Some case studies do not list alternative responses but instead describe a problem and participants are asked to respond to a series of questions that would lead to a recommendation, decision, or action plan.

2. The Action Maze is a specialized form of the case study and involves more preparation. Participants respond to the printed case study and select the option they think they should take. The facilitator gives out a printed explanation of the consequence of that chosen option. Next the group decides what they would do with the second set of options, which is followed by another consequences sheet...and so forth.

3. Another specialized form of the case study is the Incident Process. Too little data is given to the participants in order for them to reach a decision, even a preliminary one. The trainer has all the information needed but only reveals it when asked the specific question. Thus participants need to learn how to ask questions correctly so that it will lead to the information they need in order to make a decision. This Incident Process approach works particularly well in classes on labor relations, grievance procedures, investigative techniques, and problem solving.

ADAPTING AND WRITING A CASE STUDY

Follow the guidelines outlined later in this book.

SOURCES

1. Write your own case study following the guidelines provided in this book. This ensures that the problems are relevant to those faced in the particular organizational setting.

2. Have participants write cases based on problems they face on the job. The control of the content certainly increases this way.

3. Many training reference books are a good place to look for case studies. As your collection grows, determine some system of filing them for easy reference. Perhaps cross reference them by objectives, size of group, and topics.

PRACTICE: WRITE A CASE STUDY

1. Write the objective(s) based on the skills and/or principles you are covering in your workshop.

2. Write a problem that illustrates the skill or principle you want to reinforce with a case study. Be sure it is realistic.

3. Decide if there will be alternative solutions from which they will choose a resolution. Write out 4–5 alternatives.

4. Decide on how participants will work on this problem. Would they first make a decision alone and then discuss it in a small group? Would you have them work on this entirely in a small group? Will they be required to reach consensus on the resolution of the problem?

5. Prepare how the case study will be introduced.

6. Write out the questions you will ask after they have worked through the case study.

METHOD 11: IN-BASKET AND CARD SORTS

Another form of simulation involves the physical manipulation of paper that contains vital information. The In-Basket exercise simulates a typical office In-Basket which contains various items needing action. The Card Sort exercise involves multiple listing various items that are sorted, grouped, and/or ranked.

These hands-on exercises increase participants' involvement and force them to put concepts into practice. Participants must draw upon their experiences and make decisions.

GUIDELINES FOR AN IN-BASKET

1. Review your sources to find an appropriate In-Basket that fits your objectives. As needed, adapt the details or write one that fits your participants' problems or those of the organization.

   The In-Basket items should be realistic, contain some conflicting demands, force decisions, and cover simple to complex problems. The goal is for the participant to process the paperwork until all the items move from the In-Basket to the Out-Basket. Usually more work is given than can be completed in the allotted time so there's an element of stress present.

2. Divide the participants into groups of four to six.

3. Explain the purpose of doing the In-Basket, distribute the materials, read the directions, and answer questions.

4. Following the directions, individuals complete the exercise alone.

5. The small groups discuss their decisions, particularly their rationale for their rankings.

6. Conduct a discussion with the total group, polling information from each group, perhaps listing important points on the flipchart. Tie the questions to the objectives of your lesson. Follow the guidelines on how to process an exercise.

GUIDELINES FOR A CARD SORT

The Card Sort items work well when there are a multiple number of options, criteria, or decisions to make. The items should be realistic and force the sorting out of data.

1. Design a Card Sort for a problem that needs sorting out. For example, a person in a career transition has several options and can't determine which direction to go. Or a project manager must sort out the various tasks that need to be done before the project can be finished and isn't sure what order they should be in. In each case the various criteria all seem important but must be ranked so order comes out of chaos.

2. Divide the participants into groups of four to six.

3. Explain the purpose of doing the Card Sort, distribute the cards, give the directions, and answer questions.

4. Following the directions, individuals complete the Card Sort alone.

5. The small groups discuss their decisions, particularly their rationale for their rankings.

6. Conduct a discussion with the total group, polling information from each group, perhaps polling the rankings on the flipchart. Tie the questions to the objectives of your lesson. Follow the guidelines on how to process an exercise.

SOURCES

1. Write your own In-Basket or Card Sort following the guidelines provided on the facing pages. This ensures that the content is relevant to the problems faced in that particular organization or by those individuals.

2. Some training reference books include examples you can use or adapt. As your collection grows, determine some system of filing the exercises for easy reference. Perhaps cross reference them by objectives, size of group and topics.

METHOD 12: ROLE PLAYS

OVERVIEW

Role plays are another hands-on method for simulating real life. The role play enacts an incident and gives participants a chance to re-examine their behavior. It allows them the opportunity to practice and experiment with new behaviors, to emphasize different viewpoints, and to receive feedback on their behavior. A role play draws upon the participants' experiences and knowledge and forces them to apply theory to practice. Their role might be more passive if they only watch a few others enact a role play. As described here, the multiple role play will increase the role of all the learners.

FIVE TYPES OF ROLE PLAYS

1. Single

The simplest role play involves two players who are asked to re-enact a problem either from a description or one that came up in a previous discussion. The advantage here is that the whole group is able to see, then discuss, the same problem. The disadvantage is that the chosen players may feel self-conscious about being the focus of attention and only those two players get to practice the behaviors.

2. Double

Each primary player has an alter ego who stands behind the player adding comments or questions during the role play that perhaps the primary player may be thinking but not saying.

The secondary players can be assigned to the role or participants can spontaneously get into the action when they think of an additional response, help out the primary player with a new idea or get that player back to reality. The facilitator may need to demonstrate this before getting others to try it.

3. Reverse

During the role play, the facilitator asks the two people to switch roles and even seats. This helps players to empathize with another's viewpoint and to share perceptions about the other person.

The facilitator needs to be sensitive about when to do a reversal. Feelings as well as content would need to be processed carefully during the de-briefing stage.

4. Rotation

During the role play, the trainer asks new participants to continue the role play. This spontaneous replacement increases the number of people in the role play and reduces the tendency for players to be embarrassed while in the spotlight. This also increases the number of different viewpoints and approaches presented.

5. Multiple

Small groups are formed and they simultaneously enact the role play. Now everyone gets a chance to practice and to get feedback. Processing may be more difficult, but the facilitator can focus on the different approaches tried in small groups to resolve the posed problem.

SELECTING A ROLE PLAY

Review your sources for an appropriate role play that fits your objectives and participants.

Many training reference books include role plays. Keep in mind these criteria when you select a role play:

Do the objectives fit what is needed?

Is it a realistic problem?

Do the characters have distinctive conflicts?

Is it clearly written?

Are there only 2–3 characters?

Are there instructions for observers?

Can it be used as is or does it need adapting?

As needed, adapt the details of the role play to fit the participants' problems or those of the organization.

ROLE PLAYS (Continued)

WRITING A ROLE PLAY

Writing your own role play ensures that the problems are relevant to those faced in that particular organization. Refer to the guidelines on writing exercise provided earlier. Keep these in mind too:

1. Choose a problem that would require only two or three characters but that have distinctive conflicts. Make sure it is a realistic problem and one that players have in their control to solve. It shouldn't be overly complicated.

2. Give each character a name, age, gender, job title, personality traits, and perspective on the problem. Each character needs to have a goal to achieve during the role play that is broad enough to allow the player to experiment with alternative behaviors.

3. Write a concise role play providing only essential information and the facts of the problem.

4. Prepare questions for the observers to think about while watching the role play that could be discussed afterwards. Questions can cover the content of the role play and/or the feelings that were generated during the role play.

SPONTANEOUS ROLE PLAYS

As participants generate problems in your group discussions or activities, use this as an opportunity for the problem to be acted out. Follow the guidelines outlined below as you move into setting up the role play.

CONDUCTING ROLE PLAYS

1. Arrange the room so that everyone can participate fully.

2. Explain the purpose and process to be used. Do this without a lot of fanfare, moving of furniture or anything that suggests a theatrical production. (See tips below on how to overcome resistance to role playing.)

3. Verbally designate roles or distribute printed descriptions of the roles and observers' handout. Answer any questions.

4. If it's a single role play, ask for volunteers to play the roles. Either give observers verbal directions or give them printed sheets to follow while they are watching. During the enactment, only intervene if a player is having difficulty, or if you want to reverse or rotate roles. Wait until the second lull in the action before ending the role play.

If it's a multiple role play, divide participants into small groups equal to the number of characters plus one observer. Allow them to do their enactment without interference. By monitoring the progress of all the groups, you can judge how much time to allot to the role play.

PROCESSING THE ROLE

1. Always conduct a feedback session that reviews and analyzes what happened in the role play.

2. Remind the observers to use the guidelines you've given them about how to give feedback.

3. Prepare open-ended questions that cover both content and feelings. Give the role players the opportunity to respond to your questions before the observers do. If you have handed out printed questions to the observers, use these for your discussion guide.

4. Never rush processing the role play. Allow at least as much time for processing the experience as it took to do it originally.

5. Ask participants to reflect upon how this role play fits into their own reality and what they can take from the exercise back to their lives.

6. After using a role play, make notes to yourself on what did and didn't work. As your collection on role plays grows, deetermine some system of filing them for easy reference. Perhaps cross reference them by objectives and topics.

OVERCOMING RESISTANCE TO ROLE PLAYING

Since many people tend to resist role playing (including many trainers), you need to take the following into account:

1. Call it by another name, like "simulation" or "reality playing."

2. Use the role playing method later in your training design when participants are more at ease.

3. Set ground rules so that the players feel safe and re-assured that the facilitator will be protecting them from inappropriate feedback.

4. Introduce the role play without fanfare but clearly explain the purpose and process that will be used.

5. Start out with the multiple role playing so everyone is involved.

6. Ask for volunteers to role play rather than selecting the players (unless the problem emerged from a particular participant).

7. Don't use players who will be inhibited by each other due to their job roles or previous conflicts.

8. Focus the process questions on the objectives of the lesson. Also give feedback using the role players' names and not their real names.

EXERCISE—ROLE PLAYS

PRACTICE: WRITE A ROLE PLAY

1. Write the objective(s) based on the skills and/or principles you are covering in your workshop.

2. Write a problem that illustrates the skill or principle you want to reinforce with a role play. Be sure it is realistic.

3. Decide on the characters who might be a part of this problem. Give them names, a place they work or live, their roles, and even an attitude. Limit the number of characters to three.

4. Write out what the non-players should be watching for.

5. Prepare how the role play will be introduced.

6. Write out the questions you will ask after the role play has been enacted.

METHOD 13: ROLE PLAYING A CASE STUDY

OVERVIEW

Using a case study and role playing together definitely increases participants' involvement and forces them to apply theory to practice.

The role-playing case study is more elaboratively designed because it involves the participants playing defined roles. Sometimes the roles spell out their names, length of time on the job, the attitude they should have and even a hidden agenda. Other simulations assign more general roles like ''You are a member of a committee...''

Participants are given a printed description of the problem situation with sufficient detail for participants to determine the appropriate action they might take.

GUIDELINES

Be sure to review the guidelines found in this book using case studies and role plays plus keep the following in mind:

1. Review your sources for an appropriate case study that includes defined roles that could be role played, but also one that fits your objectives. As needed, adapt the details of the case study or write one that fits your participants' problems or those of the organization.

2. Divide the participants into the size of the group that fits the number of characters in the role play.

3. Explain the purpose of the activity and review the directions and roles.

4. Participants follow the directions, play out the defined roles, and make the decision(s) called for in the case.

5. Conduct a discussion with the total group gathering information on the decisions made in each group. Ask process questions that tie into the objectives of your lesson.

SOURCES

1. Write your own case study with defined roles that can be enacted. This ensures that the problems are relevant to the problems faced in that particular organization.

2. Some training reference books are a source for these case studies that include roles: adapt them to fit your objectives. As your collection of case studies grows, determine some system of filing them for easy reference. Perhaps cross reference them by objectives, size of group and topics.

METHOD 14: GAMES AND OTHER STRUCTURED ACTIVITIES

OVERVIEW

Games are another form of simulation but generally with a more competitive element to them. There are also games and other structured activities that do not depend upon competition at all.

In games and structured activities, participants are actively involved and use all their senses, which increases their energy. They help participants learn a concept or key idea, increase self awareness, provide practice for risk-taking, or develop a specific skill.

Games and structured activities range from the very simple, like ''Connect the Dots,'' to more complex ones, like ''Win as Much as You Can.''

GUIDELINES

1. Review your sources for an appropriate game or structured activity that fits your objectives. As needed, adapt the details or write one that fits your participants' problems or those of the organization.

2. Prepare the room and divide the participants into the size of the group that the directions call for.

3. Explain the purpose of the activity and review the directions.

4. Participants complete the exercise, game, or activity.

5. Conduct the process session using questions that tie into the objectives of your lesson.

SOURCES

1. Write your own game or structured activity following the guidelines provided earlier.

2. There are some training reference books for games and structured activities in the mail order catalogs.

An excellent source of non-competitive games is *Playfair* by Matt Weinstein and Joel Goodman (Impact Publishers).

EXERCISE—GAMES AND OTHER STRUCTURED ACTIVITIES

PRACTICE: ADAPTING A GAME OR STRUCTURED ACTIVITY

1. Identify your objectives for using a structured activity or game at some point in your workshop. How receptive will your participants be to a game?

2. Compare what you've diagnosed in step one with an activity or game you are considering using. What doesn't quite fit your diagnosis and objectives? Note which parts could be re-written or adapted.

3. Re-write those parts and details. Either expand or reduce parts to fit the time you have alloted for this activity.

4. Try it out, evaluate its effectivenss and re-write as needed.

METHOD 15: CLINICS

OVERVIEW

The content for the Clinic method is determined by the participant more than any of the other training methods. Participants are very active in the learning experience and have a hands-on opportunity to apply theory using this method.

CLINICS

Often, information on specific real-life problems are revealed during case studies, role plays or other methods you've used. When there is a common problem facing the group members, the Clinic is the method used to apply problem-solving techniques to analyze and resolve the problem.

The problem must be perceived as realistic and relevant to participants' jobs or lives. Even though the goal is to find solutions and develop a plan of action, the goal is also to use this as another learning experience for the participants.

This method requires the more difficult skill of facilitation. It draws upon your ability to listen, observe, question, and give feedback.

PRACTICE: List some topics that would lend themselves well to the Clinic Method:

1.

2.

3.

Write out how you would introduce this method:

METHOD 16: THE CRITICAL INCIDENTS

OVERVIEW

Like a Clinic, Critical Incidents involve participants more than any of the other methods. Because of the personal nature of Critical Incidents, great care must be taken in the planning stage to ensure the final effect is positive.

CRITICAL INCIDENTS

The Critical Incident is a more personalized and individualized form of the clinic. Actual participant experiences are the basis of this method.

Participants share a critical incident in their lives—either a career or personal event that significantly impacted their attitudes and behaviors. This information is another source of learning for the group members who can relate to or generalize from what is shared. The purpose, unlike the Clinic, is to share and validate the experience, not to solve a problem.

When many participants share their critical incidents, the others learn from a larger source than if the facilitator alone provides examples.

This method requires careful planning on how to build trust so that participants will be willing to share these significant events. It also depends on your sensitivity to the participants' feelings, ability to draw out appropriate details and help participants learn from these critical incidents.

PRACTICE: List some topics that would lend themselves well to the Critical Incident Method:

1. _____

2. _____

3. _____

Write out how you would introduce this method:

_____

_____

METHOD 17: STRUCTURED CLOSURE ACTIVITIES

OVERVIEW

Ending your workshop is just as essential as starting it off right. Planning meaningful activities for the end of the training design ensures that the participants reflect upon what they've learned and determine how they will put their goals into action.

Like structured warm-up activities, the content for these closing activities is planned by you. Participants are actively involved and appreciate the opportunity to bring closure to their learning experience.

GUIDELINES

Review your sources for an appropriate structured activity that fits your workshop objectives. As needed, adapt the details or write one that fits what your participants experienced in the workshop. See page 25.

2. Prepare the room and divide the participants into the size of the group that the directions call for.

3. Explain the purpose of the activity and review the directions.

4. Participants complete the activity.

SOURCES

1. Write your own activity following the guidelines provided in this book.

2. *Saying Goodbye: Ending Your Group Experience,* by Lois B. Hart, Leadership Dynamics, $34.95

PRACTICE: ADAPTING A CLOSURE ACTIVITY

1. Identify your objectives for a closure activity.

2. Compare what you've diagnosed in step one with an activity or game you are considering using for closure. What doesn't quite fit your objectives and time available? Note which parts could be re-written so that participants could relate better to them.

3. Re-write those parts and details. Either expand or reduce parts to fit the time you have alloted for this activity.

4. Try it out, evaluate its effectiveness and re-write as needed.

SELF ASSESSMENT

Now that you have read about and tried out some of these training methods, re-evaluate yourself:

1. Evaluate your level of expertise on each of the seventeen methods:

	I still need to learn more about this one	I understand this method but need to practice it some more	I know this so well that I could teach it!
STRUCTURED WARM-UP ACTIVITY			
PRESENTATION			
READING			
DEMONSTRATION			
VIDEO/FILM			
NOTE-TAKING			
DISCUSSION			
QUESTIONNAIRES			
FISHBOWL			
CASE STUDY			
IN-BASKET/ CARD SORT			
ROLE PLAY			
ROLE PLAY A CASE STUDY			
GAMES			
CLINICS			
CRITICAL INCIDENTS			
STRUCTURED CLOSURE ACTIVITY			

2. Check each of the following relative to how well you could do each now:

	Level of Expertise		
	None	Some	Expert
How to apply adult learning principles to methods			
How to select the most appropriate methods			
How to process activities			
How to adapt exercises			
How to write exercises			
How to judge timing			
How to evaluate methods			
How to apply methods to one of my workshops			

NOTES

FOR OTHER FIFTY-MINUTE SELF-STUDY BOOKS
SEE THE BACK OF THIS BOOK.

ABOUT THE FIFTY-MINUTE SERIES

We hope you enjoyed this book and found it valuable. If so, we have good news for you. This title is part of the best selling *FIFTY-MINUTE Series* of books. All other books are similar in size and identical in price. Several books are supported with a training video. These are identified by the symbol **V** next to the title.

Since the first *FIFTY-MINUTE* book appeared in 1986, more than five million copies have been sold worldwide. Each book was developed with the reader in mind. The result is a concise, high quality module written in a positive, readable self-study format.

FIFTY-MINUTE Books and Videos are available from your distributor or from Crisp Publications, Inc., 95 First Street, Los Altos, CA 94022. A free current catalog is available on request.

The complete list of *FIFTY-MINUTE Series* Books and Videos are listed on the following pages and organized by general subject area.

CUSTOMER SERVICE/SALES TRAINING (CONT.)

SMALL BUSINESS/FINANCIAL PLANNING

ADULT LITERACY/BASIC LEARNING

CAREER BUILDING

To order books/videos from the **FIFTY-MINUTE** Series, please:

1. **CONTACT YOUR DISTRIBUTOR**

   or

2. **Write to Crisp Publications, Inc.**
   95 First Street   (415) 949-4888 - phone
   Los Altos, CA 94022   (415) 949-1610 - FAX